CRIMINAL RESPONSIBILITY

By Lord Loveday Ememe and available at Lulu and Amazon
The constitution and policing
Heresy
Starfleet
The Supernatural
Creation
Deterrence
Stalking
The media
Adam

www.lulu.com
Copyright© Lord Loveday Ememe 2013
The author asserts the moral right to be recognized as the author of this work.
ISBN: 978-1-291-44864-1

Table of Contents

1. What are the possibilities with the use of supernatural powers and senses in order to determine criminal responsibility?
2. Criminal conspiracy
3. Criminal intent
4. Author's notes
5. Author's biography
6. Bibliography

1. What are the possibilities with the use of supernatural powers and senses in order to determine criminal responsibility?

The bible or the civil constitution of man defines a crime as the misuse of supernatural powers and senses by the uncivilized with supernatural powers and senses to harm mentally or physically the civilized without supernatural powers and senses or to breach the peace in a civilized society.

A crime is established by measuring the effects of supernaturalism on the civil constitution. A civilized society is established if that society is under the dominion of the civilized. The civilized is defined by the bible as a person or persons without supernatural powers and senses. A supernatural is defined by the constitution or bible as a person with supernatural powers and senses. A crime is committed by a supernatural when supernatural powers and senses are misused to harm the civilized mentally or physically, whether the supernatural was pretending to be civilized or not during the commission of the crime. When a supernatural pretends to be civilized during the commission of a crime, it does not absorb the supernatural of the crime, the same way if an armed robber robs a bank while wearing a mask, the mask does not absorb the robber of the crime when caught with the mask. If a supernatural thinks pretending to be civilized will absorb him or her of a crime, they will get a spot on the television show called America's dumbest criminals.

The extent of supernatural powers and senses, meaning the possibilities regarding their uses help establish whether a crime has been committed or the magnitude or seriousness of a crime, given the constitutional rights of the civil constitution.

The civil constitution has a natural adverse reaction to lawlessness confirming that the civil constitution is severely mentally impaired of intelligence for unlawful social functioning. It is necessary to note that supernaturalism, direct or indirect is unlawful.

The nobility in the United Kingdom have tried to model its way of life on the civil constitution but with necessary legal or moral limitations as a consequence of their supernatural constitutions.

The nobility believe correctly that there should be a distinction made between a noble and the working class, a noble should be educated separately as a noble, ready always for command and to govern. The nobility also believe that there should not be informal relationships between the nobility and the working class. What they failed to mention is that informality is impossible with the civil constitution. The likes and dislikes of the civil constitution are the laws of the planet, which are referred to as ministering. The civil constitution has a sacred objectivity as a consequence of not having supernatural powers and senses. It serves no purposes to try to manipulate the sacred findings of the civil constitution because it will undermine law and order.

The nobility requires the working class to always address the nobility formally using their official titles. The nobility of lesser ranks are always required to address the senior nobles formally to set a proper example for the working class, which helps establish and maintain law and order.

The education, healthcare, companionship etcetera of a noble is different from that of the working class, contrary to the misconception of its fairness, its moral justification is derived from the differences in the constitutions of a real noble, the civil constitution and the real working class, the supernatural constitution.

Contrary to the misconception, the monarch and the nobility are sacrifices of families to model their lives on the civil constitution in order to establish and maintain law and order within the moral and legal limitations of the supernatural constitution, although these sacrifices are being undermined by politics and political supernatural lawless activities. These legal and moral limitations on the nobility as a consequence of the supernatural constitution expressed in the United Kingdom national anthem, God Save the Queen, are easily corrected by a real law lord as the real representation of Christianity or the law. This simply requires the proper implementation of the law including the proper installation of the real law lords, the civilized, as commissioners of the metropolitan (civilization) police force. The real command structure in law enforcement puts the law first, as the law commissions the queen to rule, who in turn commissions a police force to establish and maintain order. The queen or monarch in the United Kingdom can only be commissioned by the law in the form of a real law lord the civilized if he or she rules or governs in line with the correct interpretation of the Christian principles, similar to swearing an oath of allegiance to uphold the law. This suggests that in a properly constituted government, the chain of command puts the law in the form of a real law lord, the civil constitution above the monarch. It is the civil constitution or civil God and not the supernatural constitution or supernatural God that commissions a supernatural monarch (coronation).

To say that someone is criminally responsible for their actions when a crime has been committed is to make a determination that they are aware of the harmful effects of their actions and that their actions are unlawful. The supernatural constitution is aware beforehand in a more detailed way of the harmful effects of their actions and that their actions are unlawful because of the supernatural powers of premonitions. As a consequence criminal responsibility exists when you can establish that a person has supernatural powers and senses regardless of their age.

It is based on this principle of criminal responsibility that the constitution, the bible or Christian principles, instructs the indiscriminate destruction and continuous suffering of the uncivilized with supernatural powers and senses. The existence of supernatural powers and senses means that the current unlawful systems of government in the world is deliberate and calculated to create hostile living conditions that caters to the sadistic nature of the supernatural constitution at the expense of law and order and the mental and physical wellbeing of the vulnerable.

According to the constitution, the bible, criminal responsibility cannot be established with the civil constitution because of the absence of supernatural powers and senses. This means that the unlawful attempts by the uncivilized by misusing their supernatural powers and senses to create false impressions of wrongdoing(sins or crimes) by the civil constitution is politically motivated to undermine the constitutional authority of the civil constitution, which is evidence of a supernatural illness I will call the dumb criminal syndrome. This dumb criminal syndrome is used to justify unprovoked attacks on the civil constitution by a supernatural.

The constitution, the bible, seems to suggest that as a consequence of the existence of supernatural powers and senses in the supernatural constitution, confirms that an unlawful system of government can only exists with the collective participation of all uncivilized people with supernatural powers and senses, this collective criminal responsibility principle suggests that the uncivilized collectively are infected with the dumb criminal syndrome, a supernatural illness.

It is inconceivable to put any limits on what is possible with the supernatural powers and senses of the supernatural constitution, which raises unanswered questions about the creation of the unlawful concept of poverty. It is blasphemy for the civil constitution to experience poverty. The civil constitution is ruler and has dominion over this planet and the supernatural constitution. This really means that the civil constitution is God and not the supernatural constitution. It is as a consequence inconceivable to put any limits on the civil powers of the civil constitution.

As a consequence of the endless possibilities of supernatural powers and senses the criminal liability of the supernatural constitution is extensive and the criminal responsibility of the supernatural constitution.

The civil powers of the civil constitution must be proportionate to the supernatural powers of the supernatural constitution in order to adequately regulate its use.

There are two types of Gods, the supernatural God and the civilized God. The civil constitution was selected to be ruler, and the civil constitution was designed specifically for the purpose of governing. The determination was made that the need for the supernatural constitution was never meant to be on-going compared to the continuous need of the law in the form of the civil constitution. The supernatural constitution rebelled against this sacred selection of the civil constitution as ruler and has been trying unlawfully to show the importance of the supernatural constitution by not completing its one-off task of creation and as a consequence has created unlawfully hell on earth.

Before colonialism most of the countries colonized had adopted a simple way of living and simple systems of government based on the civil constitution. This simple system of government was used in Europe centuries ago. The political supernatural system they have been replaced with has unlawfully created hell on earth. The unusual interest in government generated by the political system is not an endorsement of the system but because of self-preservation because of the terrorizing nature of the political system. The political system is an attempt to legalize terrorism. The political system is a representation of the supernatural constitution. The supernatural constitution is political by nature.

The supernatural constitution does not have the patience or temperament to govern. They will always want to abuse their position to create activities to cater to their supernatural constitution which will undermine or compromise their ability to govern. Governing under these illegal political supernatural systems is humiliating as they struggle to make the pointless supernatural political system compatible with a simple process of governing. The supernatural constitution is always surplus to requirement with most civilized activities and in order to fit in they destroy the activities rather than leave them for those they are meant for.

It is possible to streamline the method of government to a very simple process to suit those governing is meant for, the civil constitution; the simple way of living is possible with reasonable advancements in technology to align the modern world with the principles developed in the Garden of Eden.

The civil constitution is created the same way a supernatural constitution is created and a law lord from birth the same way the supernatural constitution is supernatural from birth.

In law enforcement an order is a decision made by the civil

constitution or under the authority of the civil constitution as supreme commander. It is an order because of the civilized nature of the civil constitution and implies that the supreme commander's decisions will be an extension of the civil constitution that is why they are called orders. That is why it is a serious crime for a supernatural to impersonate the civilized for the purpose of issuing sacred orders as this will undermine universal peace and security.

When in law enforcement, the military and the current illegitimate supernatural governments, orders are issued; they are being done in the name of the god of laws, the civil constitution, they are fraudulent because they are operating illegally outside the guidelines of the real constitution. They are operating fraudulently outside the guidelines of the constitution without the essential requirement of the constitution which insists that the civilized must be officially identified as law lords(supreme court judges and commissioners of police) with rights, privileges and official salaries, and any supernatural trying to use the law, for example assistance with law enforcement must first be required to take an oath to uphold the law by identifying, interpreting and applying the law correctly.   The civil constitution is protected under any circumstances, according to the constitution the bible or Christian principles a lawless system should only affect the security of the supernatural constitution and not the civil constitution. This is because the constitution of this planet has correctly determined that the nature of the supernatural constitution means that criminal responsibility applies to the uncivilized collectively because of their supernatural powers and senses in a lawless system of government. The constitution has correctly determined that in a lawless system the uncivilized collectively have allowed the constitutional authority of the civil constitution to be undermined unlawfully.

The constitution, the bible or Christian principles, has correctly made a determination that the criminal responsibility principle cannot apply to the civil constitution because of the lack of supernatural powers and senses.

This means that when the uncivilized harm mentally or physically the civil constitution as if retaliating when a determination has already been made by the constitution that the civil constitution cannot be criminally responsible because of the lack of supernatural powers and senses, then the attacks will be categorized by the constitution as treason.

Because international and domestic laws have been enacted unlawfully by the uncivilized pretending to be civilized, they do not authorize the supernatural constitution to have contact with the civil constitution using these laws. It appears to be alright to use them because the uncivilized use them amongst themselves, these legislations do not recognize the supernatural constitution so anything could appear to be permitted while role playing or acting, role play or acting is how the supernatural constitution interact with each other. Role play or acting is possible for the supernatural constitution but beyond the natural capabilities of the civil constitution. The laws governing role play or acting requires all parties involved to consent beforehand and to know beforehand what will happen similar to a movie script and no one should be harmed mentally or physically in the process. This is clearly possible for the supernatural constitution because of supernatural powers and senses but beyond the natural capabilities of the civil constitution because of the lack of supernatural powers and senses. None of these laws authorizes the supernatural constitution contact with the civil constitution, once these laws are applied to the civil constitution they become active because they recognize the civil constitution and will immediately interpret the actions of the supernatural constitution as fraudulent. This will suggest that any communication from the civil constitution under these laws should be taken by the supernatural constitution as commands.

2. Criminal conspiracy

CRIMINAL RESPONSIBILITY

The principle of criminal responsibility requires those that knowingly commit crimes should be brought to justice in the interest of peace and security. This principle when applied correctly to the supernatural constitution has a wider net that implicates the uncivilized collectively because of the possibilities of supernatural powers and senses. This is in line with the constitution's instructions for the continuous suffering of the wicked and the indiscriminate destruction of the wicked. The nature of the supernatural constitution means that the uncivilized cannot pretend that they are unaware of the unlawful persecution of the righteous, law lords.

The supernatural constitution's ability to see into the future extends the net of criminal responsibility.

Your mental capacity, what you know, how you know, when you knew, are essential components in establishing criminal responsibility. These components also establish criminal conspiracy.

The current lawless supernatural system in place means that the righteous, the civilized, are severely mentally impaired of intelligence for this type of lawless supernatural political social functioning. The care needs of the civilized under these circumstances are the immediate correction of the lawless system and the implementation of a lawful system.

The audacity of a supernatural to violate the civil rights of the righteous, the civil constitution, is as a consequence of the collective conspiracy of the uncivilized to unlawfully persecute those different from them. Prevention is better than cure. The supernatural constitution is capable of preventing mental and physical attacks on their real rulers the civil constitution before it happens. This is the reason the constitution automatically deems the supernatural constitution criminally responsible and a criminal conspiracy when the civil constitution is supernaturally attacked.

The nobility requires a noble to be made aware of the differences between a noble and the working class from the beginning of the noble's education, and the noble must be educated separately as a noble. The education must be tailored to the noble's status. Although for political reasons the traditional education of a noble is being compromised. The education must be done privately and a noble should not be educated with the working class. The nobles are the civil constitution and the working class the supernatural constitution. The nobles are traditionally not allowed to socialize with the working class because the working class are seen as uncivilized and a corrupting influence on a noble and in some cases extremely unhealthy for the noble. This is confirmed by the bible with the relationships between the supernatural and civil constitutions. The supernatural constitution traditionally wants to undermine unlawfully the sacred constitutional authority of the civil constitution.

Promotions in law enforcement is political for the supernatural political constitution, unlike the civil constitution, it is the action or behaviour of the supernatural constitution that determines whether they are good or bad, the civil constitution is good by nature. This is why the civil constitution is supreme commander and the supernatural constitution aspires to the natural qualities or characteristics of the civil constitution in law enforcement.

The supernatural constitution always makes the fatal mistake of trying to communicate politically supernaturally with the civil legal constitution which is unhealthy and beyond the natural capabilities of the civil constitution.

As someone who is of a civil constitution and a real noble, my education was compromised by the uncivilized whose judgements were compromised and influenced by their uncivilized constitutions, my educational development was self-taught, as I can only rely on myself to learn how to be a real nobleman. I was educated in the ways of the supernatural constitution which is beyond the natural capabilities of the civil constitution. The education was not compatible with my civil constitution. The undermining of my natural development could only have been possible by the collective criminal conspiracy of the uncivilized.

CRIMINAL RESPONSIBILITY

The unlawful system in place in the world that persecutes those different from the uncivilized, the vulnerable, including the civilized or the law serves another retaliatory purpose of being a constant humiliation for the creators, the uncivilized. This poses additional problems for their victims, the vulnerable, because the unlawful system exposes the desperation of the supernatural constitution, to create unlawfully hell on earth, in order to eliminate boredom by creating lawless social activities. This includes exploiting the needs of the vulnerable to unlawfully put themselves in your way by creating a lawless supernatural social activity. The more apparent their desperation the more they look for ways to try to humiliate their victims because their victims are aware of the desperation of the supernatural constitution to humiliate themselves in order to eliminate boredom. This desperation of the supernatural constitution is responsible for the undermining of law and order. In order to establish and maintain law and order there can be no compromises that cater to the supernatural constitution, the uncivilized will have to learn to exercise self-control and learn how to be supernatural within the law.

The uncivilized have collectively conspired through action or inaction to give names to the misuse of their supernatural powers and senses by referring to them as naturally occurring illnesses or diseases like aids, cancer, flesh eating bugs, foot and mouth disease etcetera. This also includes other abuses of power referred to as naturally occurring disasters like famine, poverty or destitution etcetera.

According to the constitution, the bible, the life spans of both the supernatural and civil constitutions were meant to be never ending, indefinite.

It is correct to say that the civilized are severely mentally impaired of intelligence for the current lawless supernatural social functioning, as a consequence the real care needs of the civil constitution is the real civil rights outlined in the Garden of Eden for Lord Adam before he was unlawfully overthrown as ruler by the conspiracy of the uncivilized.

CRIMINAL RESPONSIBILITY

The uncivilized psychopaths want me to pretend that I like their unhealthy unlawful supernatural social activities; I am actually being bullied by the uncivilized psychopaths into going along with activities or processes that are beyond the natural capabilities of the civil constitution.

If you are different from these uncivilized psychopaths you are persecuted as if deformed because they do not want to let go of the official roles meant for the civil constitution similar to Hitler and the Nazis' attitude towards those they considered deformed or disabled. The constitution or bible requires the use of supernatural powers and senses to police those capable of committing crimes, the uncivilized or supernatural constitution. The civilized are not capable of committing crimes because of the lack of supernatural powers and senses. Committing crimes are beyond the natural capabilities of the civil constitution. This also explains the harmful effects of direct or indirect supernaturalism on the civil constitution.

Contrary to misconceptions or false impressions the church is a different interpretation of the Christian faith from the monarchy in the United Kingdom. The church represents supernaturalism or lawlessness and the monarchy represents the civil constitution or law and order.

I am of a civilized constitution, which means that I have no supernatural powers and senses. I became aware that those around me including family were of supernatural constitutions in 2000/2001, which means that they have supernatural powers and senses. After about 28 years of concealing their true identities from me, at the same time advocating practices and lifestyles while pretending to be civilized that were unhealthy for the real civil constitution and beyond the natural capabilities of the civil constitution. Although they are still reluctant to admit the differences at the expense of my mental and physical wellbeing I am aware it exists. They are sadistically making me take medication as if I am hallucinating and as if the differences do not exist. Even after telling me years ago that there was no cure for the hallucinations. Moses, King Solomon, King David, Abraham etcetera were all hallucinating if you believe the criminal conspiracy of the uncivilized.

The method of socializing for the supernatural constitution is based on hostilities which are beyond the natural capabilities of the civil constitution. The uncivilized, based on their hostile form of interaction or socializing force things on you, things you do not want or you have already rejected. This is the way they sadistically supernaturally plan the lives of those different from them that are defenceless without supernatural powers and senses. The nature of the supernatural constitution will suggest that these sadistic practices are only possible with the collective participation of the uncivilized. This helps define the reach of criminal responsibility when applied to the supernatural constitution.

Jesus Christ was betrayed and was denied recognition by his disciples which led to torture imprisonment and death. These are the characteristics of the supernatural constitution pretending to be civilized. The civil constitution should be concerned when the uncivilized claim to be friends, their method of friendship will lead to fatalities. The injuries or fatalities will be to their so-called friends.

My movements have been restricted because I have been made to get lost by the misuse of supernatural powers and senses. When I use the train it is made to move at angles that defies the laws of physics by the deliberate misuse of supernatural powers and senses by the uncivilized. These attacks can only be achieved by the collective conspiracy of the uncivilized.

It is implied in the current criminal justice system that if you see a crime in progress or the abuse of a vulnerable person or persons it is your duty as a citizen of a country of the international community to report it to the proper authority or authorities. You also must have a proper understanding of what actions, behaviour or practices constitute a crime or crimes. The nature of the supernatural constitution means that it is impossible for the uncivilized not to know beforehand that a crime is about to take place. This ability of the supernatural constitution helps define the reach of criminal responsibility of the supernatural constitution in relation to aiding and abating or criminal conspiracy. As a natural law lord, a commissioner of the metropolitan police force, I can only commission a properly constituted police force that keeps real peace and fights real crimes as defined by the real constitution, the bible.

On this basis as a citizen of the United Kingdom and a real law lord, I have appointed myself a commissioner of the metropolitan police force as I only know of me to be someone of a civil constitution with the sacred legitimacy to do it.

The uncivilized wrongly believe that the more of them that participate in making a decision or judgement will give the decision or judgement legitimacy. The only reason to get political in making decisions or judgements is if they do not have legitimacy.

The American criminal justice system requires evidence to be obtained legally to be admissible in court. This is because of the principle or doctrine of law enforcement that the criminal justice system must be good and operate legally. Rules of evidence in the American criminal justice system rules out the possibility of the supernatural constitution investigating the civil constitution for committing a crime or crimes as the real constitution considers it impossible for the civil constitution to commit crimes. The attempts at honesty of the American criminal justice system rules in the possibility of policing properly supernaturally (including investigations) the uncivilized that are capable of committing crimes because of their supernatural powers and senses.

When the uncivilized approach the civilized illegally everything resulting from the unlawful approach is invalid. In some cases the uncivilized do this deliberately with issues involving confirmation of the official role of the civil constitution as law lords to undermine the constitutional authority of the civil constitution as law lords.

The uncivilized believe that the end justifies the supernatural dramatic lawless means. These means are beyond the natural capabilities of the civil constitution.

It is the dumb criminal syndrome that will make the uncivilized allow themselves to be drawn into a criminal conspiracy to undermine law and order and the civil constitution. The sacrificial nature of the civil constitution means that the supernatural constitution owes the civil constitution a duty of care, the criminal responsibility of the supernatural constitution is linked to the duty of care to ensure the establishment and maintenance of peace and security. The care needs of the civil constitution are the real civil rights as outlined in the real constitution. These civil rights are really a monarch or ruler's rights; you must be of a civil constitution to have these rights.

3. Criminal intent

To establish criminal intent the person or persons must have supernatural powers and senses. The uncivilized are rigging everything including education to make sure that everyone falls below the required moral standards. As this is impossible to achieve with the civil constitution the civil constitution becomes a challenge for the supernatural constitution which unlawfully makes life hell for the civil constitution.

The uncivilized do not quite understand that the history of the United Kingdom with regard to the nobility and the working class is a distinction between the civil constitution and the supernatural constitution. The civil constitution is nobility and the supernatural constitution is the working class. The nobility in the United Kingdom have been accused of not wanting to socialize with the working as if it is a bad thing, snobbery, without the true facts of the unhealthy nature of the supernatural constitution on the civil constitution and in a civilized society. There are a lot of different ways the civilized are being protected from the unhealthy effects of direct or indirect supernaturalism unsuccessfully, the data protection laws, rights to privacy etcetera, because of the natural behavioural problems of the supernatural constitution. The only way to properly protect the civil constitution is to identify, interpret and apply the real constitution correctly.

The supernatural constitution bears the type of grudge a criminal or terrorist bears against the state or the law and the civil constitution bears the type of grudge the law or state bears against a criminal or terrorist for the purposes of law and order or peace and security. It is on this basis that they have developed their own unlawful version of retaliations against the state or civil constitution.

The uncivilized and their disease the dumb criminal syndrome believe that they are helping the civil constitution rather than themselves with the creation of a lawful system of government. A lawless system of government makes the uncivilized collectively bastards and idiots. They are not recognized as a person or persons under the law in a lawless system of government because of their supernatural powers and senses.

To establish intent in the commission of a crime, the person must know that what they are doing is wrong and the resulting effects or consequences of their actions. This is always going to be present with the supernatural constitution. The supernatural constitution because of its supernatural powers and senses knows for certain the effects or consequences of its actions.

The work concept compatible with the constitutional role of the civil constitution is the old style administration by the nobility over seven hundred years ago before the creation of the House of Commons in parliament in the United Kingdom. It is compatible with the old style type of administration in African countries over three hundred years ago. These old style administrations are relevant in the modern world given the differences in the civil and supernatural constitutions.

As someone of a civil constitution I have a civilized interest in things like women, money, films, books, music etcetera. These interests have been turned unlawfully into supernatural interests that are beyond the natural capabilities of the civil constitution by the uncivilized stalking me supernaturally.

A properly constituted police force headed by the civilized in line with the instructions of the real constitution, the bible, must have uniforms that signify a uniformity of purpose despite the differences, to protect the differences, individuality, personal freedoms and independence.

Your mental capacity is used to determine or establish criminal responsibility or criminal intent, the mental capacity of the supernatural constitution is enormous as a consequence of their supernatural powers and senses which automatically establish criminal responsibility and criminal intent when a crime is committed. A supernatural that causes mental or physical harm to the civilized while pretending or role playing is committing a serious crime. The nature of the supernatural constitution will establish criminal intent. Also because the civil and supernatural constitutions are not compatible for jokes, games or socializing, criminal intent will be established when mental or physical harm is caused to the civil constitution as consequence.

As a consequence of the potentially dangerous nature of the supernatural constitution confirms that contact with the civil constitution can never be informal or voluntary.

Because of the lawless political nature of the supernatural constitution they believe wrongly that the more of them there are in a decision making process or judgement the fairer the decision or judgement. This is a political rather than a legal way of thinking. If you are righteous or behaving righteously you do not need the backing of others to validate your decision or judgement. Uncivilized psychopaths make decisions or judgements for political emotional reasons rather than for legal purposes.

The uncivilized have a natural stubborn behavioural trait which some of them mistakenly associate with the civil constitution.

An angel is a supernatural directly under the charge of the law or civil constitution.

If the monarchy needs help policing, the problem can be resolved with a concept similar to jury duty amongst the uncivilized.

When the uncivilized undermine the chain of command in law enforcement by not officially acknowledging the constitutional authority of the civil constitution, it is unconstitutional, the purpose of a chain of command in law enforcement is to protect the civil constitution as supreme commanders and to establish discipline within law enforcement which then establishes and maintains law and order. To undermine law and order within law enforcement will be categorized as dumb criminal syndrome.

International and domestic laws do not recognize the supernatural constitution for purposes of contact with the civil constitution that is recognized as a person. This lack of recognition of the supernatural constitution is also for health and safety purposes for the protection of the civil constitution. To pretend to be a person under these laws for the purposes of contact with the civil constitution is fraudulent, a crime against humanity. It also falls under the category of the dumb criminal syndrome, given the reach of criminal responsibility when

CRIMINAL RESPONSIBILITY

applied to the supernatural constitution because of its mental capacity as consequence of its supernatural powers and senses. The civil constitution is not hostile or aggressive given the differences in the civil and supernatural constitutions; it is beyond the natural capabilities of the civil constitution. The civil constitution is naturally allergic to real lawlessness, even when the parties involved are not aware that their actions are unlawful, although lack of awareness of the harmful effects of their actions is impossible given the nature of the supernatural constitution. These natural allergies could manifest in different forms. My experiences of the misuse of supernatural powers and senses by the supernatural constitution will suggest that the uncivilized way animals in the wild live; killing each other for food must be attributed to supernatural interference. They have been interfered with supernaturally.

Age is not a barrier for a noble to be identified or acknowledged as ruler or monarch. If too young, the noble will be identified as ruler, landlord or monarch but someone older will take over the administrative affairs temporarily until the noble reaches maturity. The uncivilized psychopaths have given names to the different ways they misuse their supernatural powers and senses, examples of the names they have given to the misuse of their supernatural powers and senses are famine, poverty, cancer, aids, flesh eating bugs, foot and mouth disease etcetera. These misuses of supernatural powers and senses make life impossible for those different from them unlawfully.

According to the real interpretation of the constitution or bible the life spans of the supernatural and civil constitutions are indefinite which means that a person that is a thousand years old is still an infant. Unlike the civil constitution being supernatural does not make you a police officer or an angel, to be a police officer or an angel a supernatural must be commissioned by a real law lord, the civil constitution.

The constitution, the bible, defines crime as the misuse of supernatural powers and senses by the uncivilized, those with supernatural powers and senses, to harm mentally or physically the civilized, those without supernatural powers and senses, and to breach the peace in a civilized society. This means that to establish criminal intent or criminal responsibility the person or persons must have supernatural powers and senses. The proper investigation of crimes requires the use of supernatural powers and senses.

4. Author's notes

CRIMINAL RESPONSIBILITY

Criminal responsibility is my tenth book about the correct identification, interpretation and application of the laws of this planet. The real constitution the bible defines crime as the misuse of supernatural powers and senses by the uncivilized, those with supernatural powers and senses, to harm mentally or physically the civilized, those without supernatural powers and senses, or to breach the peace in a civilized society.

This means that to establish criminal intent or criminal responsibility the person or persons must have supernatural powers and senses.

It is baffling how the uncivilized have conspired collectively to undermine the law in the form of the civil constitution by creating false impressions that the civil constitution the law could be criminally responsible contrary to the guidelines of the real constitution the bible.

5. Author's biography

CRIMINAL RESPONSIBILITY

My name is Lord Loveday Ememe. I was born in the United Kingdom. I am a graduate of an Anglican seminary school. I also graduated from the University of East London with an honours degree in law. I am of a civilized constitution.

6. Bibliography

The Bible

www.ingramcontent.com/pod-product-compliance
Lightning Source LLC
Chambersburg PA
CBHW072305170526
45158CB00003BA/1197